APR   2012

I WANT TO KNOW ABOUT
Reptiles

by Dee Phillips

NEW
FOREST
PRESS

I WANT TO KNOW ABOUT
Reptiles

Publisher: Tim Cook   Editor: Valerie J. Weber   Designer: Matt Harding

ISBN 978 1 84898 524 7
Library of Congress Control Number: 2011924960

U.S. publication © 2011 New Forest Press
Published in arrangement with Black Rabbit Books

PO Box 784, Mankato, MN 56002

www.newforestpress.com
Printed in the USA
15 14 13 12 11 1 2 3 4 5

Picture Credits:
(t=top, b=bottom, c=center, l=left, r=right)
Alamy: 15. Shutterstock: Front cover, 1, 2, 3 (all), 5 (all), 6b, 8b, 9, 10b, 12b, 13, 14 (all), 16b, 17, 18b, 19, 20b, 22b, 23, 24 (all), 25, 26b, 28b, 29, back cover. ticktock Media Archive: 4, 6c, 7, 8c, 10c, 11, 12c, 16c, 18c, 20c, 21, 22c, 26c, 27, 28c.

CONTENTS

REPTILES

Words that appear in **bold** are defined in the glossary.

A World of Reptiles

Reptiles live almost everywhere in the world, except in very cold places. Most live in hot, humid places. They are cold-blooded and cannot make their own body heat. Reptiles depend on the temperature of the air around them to stay warm. All reptiles have a back bone. Most have four legs, except for **snakes**. **Scales** cover reptiles' dry skin.

Some reptiles live on many different **continents**. Others live in lots of places on just one continent. Some reptiles live in only one country, such as Madagascar or Mexico. When you read about an animal, see if you can find the place where it lives on the map below. You can also look for the part of the world where you live.

This world map shows the continents in bold uppercase letters and countries in bold lowercase letters.

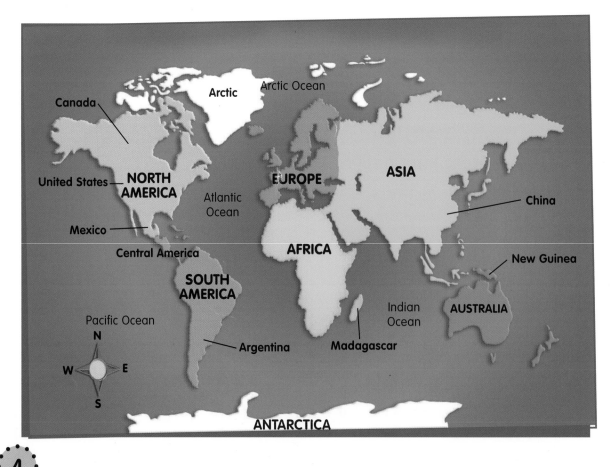

Where Do Reptiles Live?

Some animals live in hot places, such as deserts. Others live in forests or in the ocean. The different types of places where animals live are called habitats.

Look for these pictures. They will show you what kind of habitat each animal lives in.

deserts: hot, dry, sandy places where it hardly ever rains

grasslands: dry places covered with grass

lakes, ponds, rivers, or streams

mountains: high, rocky places

oceans: vast areas of water

rain forests: warm forests with lots of rain

seashores: land along the edges of oceans and seas

temperate forests: cool forests with trees that lose their leaves in winter

What Do Reptiles Eat?

Some reptiles eat only meat, fish, bugs, or spiders. Others eat only plants. Many amphibians eat both other animals and plants. Look for these pictures to tell you what kind of food each animal eats.

bugs or spiders

fish

invertebrates

meat

plants

snails and shellfish

Alligator

Alligators live in **swamps**, rivers, and lakes in the southeastern United States and eastern China. They hunt for fish, snakes, turtles, lizards, and birds.

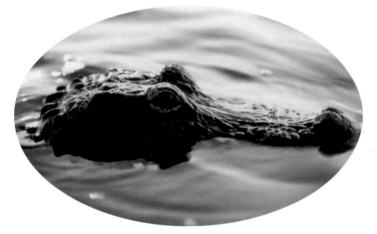

An alligator's eyes and **nostrils** stick up above the water. They can see above the surface of the water. Even with its body underwater, it can still see and smell its **prey**.

Alligators hiss, bellow, and grunt. Baby alligators can call to their mothers when they are in danger.

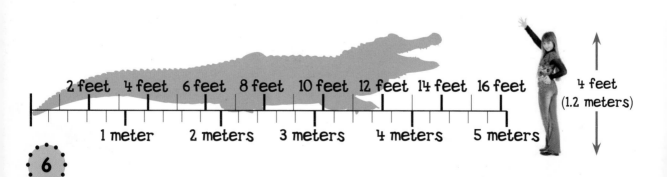

2 feet   4 feet   6 feet   8 feet   10 feet   12 feet   14 feet   16 feet

1 meter   2 meters   3 meters   4 meters   5 meters

4 feet
(1.2 meters)

Its powerful tail pushes the alligator through the water.

Alligators use their sharp teeth to grab their prey, not to chew it. If they lose a tooth, they can regrow it.

Bearded Dragon

The bearded dragon is a kind of **lizard**. It lives in forests and hot, dry places in Australia.

Bearded dragons feed on plants, fruit, and flowers. They also hunt insects, **rodents**, and other lizards for food.

Females lay their eggs in sandy ground. The babies **hatch** out on their own.

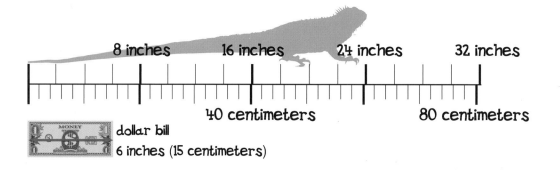

8 inches   16 inches   24 inches   32 inches

40 centimeters   80 centimeters

dollar bill
6 inches (15 centimeters)

Sometimes bearded dragons sit on branches or fences to guard their **territory**. Sometimes they dig a hole underground. There, they can avoid the heat.

Scales stick out like **spikes** from a pouch on its throat. The bearded dragon can make this pouch grow bigger to scare off **predators**.

Black Mamba

Black mambas are deadly snakes that live in eastern and southern Africa. Their **poison** can kill a person in twenty minutes.

But they usually hunt small **mammals** and birds. They bite their prey with long, sharp **fangs**.

Black mambas often slide into cracks in rocks to live. Sometimes they climb quickly into trees.

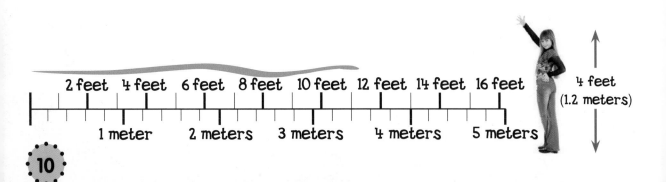

2 feet 4 feet 6 feet 8 feet 10 feet 12 feet 14 feet 16 feet

1 meter 2 meters 3 meters 4 meters 5 meters

4 feet
(1.2 meters)

The black mamba is not actually black. Its skin can be dark green, brown, or gray.

A female mamba lays her eggs underground. The baby snakes hatch out and can begin to hunt right away.

Chameleon

Chameleons are lizards with special skin.
When a chameleon gets scared or excited,
its skin changes colors.

A chameleon's tongue
shoots out so fast that
you cannot see it. It is
twice as long as the
chameleon's body.

Its tail can hold onto branches.

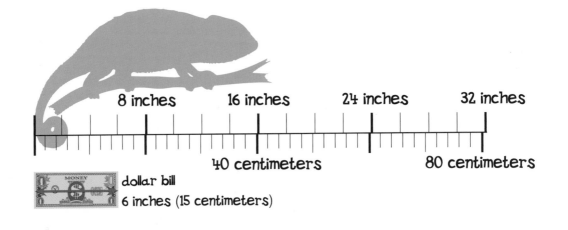

8 inches   16 inches   24 inches   32 inches

40 centimeters   80 centimeters

dollar bill
6 inches (15 centimeters)

This Ambilobe panther chameleon comes from Madagascar.

Chameleons have excellent eyesight. One eye can look forward, while the other eye is looking backward.

Cobra

Cobras are snakes that live in many different habitats in southern Asia and southern Africa. They are very **poisonous**.

A cobra can spread the ribs in its neck to form a hood. When it meets a predator, it partly rises and spreads the hood.

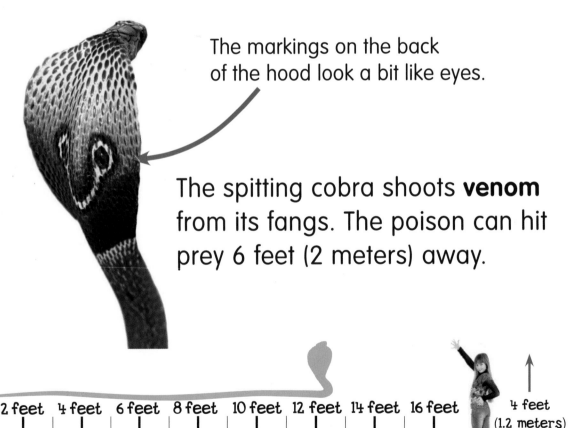

The markings on the back of the hood look a bit like eyes.

The spitting cobra shoots **venom** from its fangs. The poison can hit prey 6 feet (2 meters) away.

2 feet 4 feet 6 feet 8 feet 10 feet 12 feet 14 feet 16 feet

1 meter 2 meters 3 meters 4 meters 5 meters

4 feet (1.2 meters)

Cobras eat rats, birds, lizards, toads, and other snakes. They swallow their prey whole, eating the head first.

Indian cobras lay about twelve to twenty eggs. The baby snakes hatch out after sixty days.

Crocodile

Crocodiles are huge predators. They live in Africa, Australia, Mexico, Southeast Asia, and Central and South America. They crawl through lakes, rivers, and swamps.

Adult crocodiles eat fish, birds, and mammals. Powerful jaws with sharp teeth snap shut on their prey. Crocodiles even eat other crocodiles' babies!

Female crocodiles lay their eggs in a hole on a sandy riverbank. They cover the hole with plants to keep it warm. Some crocodiles even lie on their eggs to warm them.

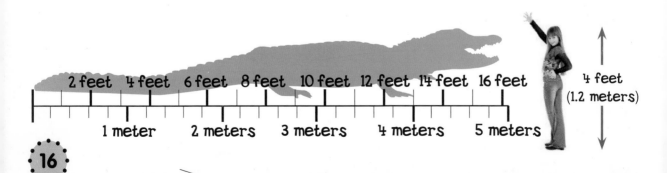

2 feet   4 feet   6 feet   8 feet   10 feet   12 feet   14 feet   16 feet

1 meter   2 meters   3 meters   4 meters   5 meters

4 feet
(1.2 meters)

Thick scales cover
a crocodile's body.

A crocodile's
eyes and nostrils
are on top of its
head. The rest of
its body can be
underwater, and
the crocodile can
still see.

Galapagos Tortoise

Tortoises are reptiles with shells. Galapagos tortoises are the biggest tortoises in the world. They live on **islands** near South America.

They like to munch on grass, **cacti**, and other plants. They also like to sunbathe and relax in muddy puddles.

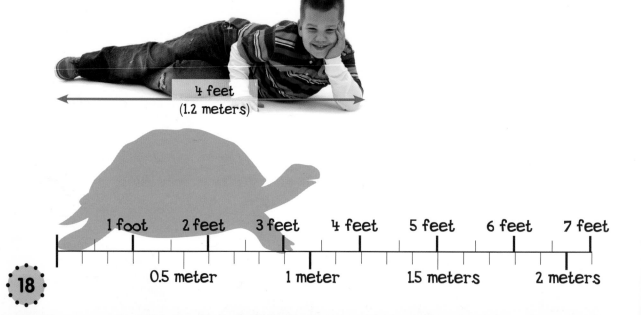

4 feet
(1.2 meters)

1 foot   2 feet   3 feet   4 feet   5 feet   6 feet   7 feet

0.5 meter   1 meter   1.5 meters   2 meters

Galapagos tortoises can grow to more than 500 pounds (227 kilograms). They can also live to more than one hundred years old.

Like other tortoises, they can pull their head and legs inside their shell.

Komodo Dragon

The huge Komodo dragon is the biggest of all the lizards. Komodo dragons live on islands near southeast Asia.

They can smell food from up to 6 miles (10 kilometers) away. They often eat other animals' leftover prey.

The Komodo can kill with its spit when it bites its prey. Poisonous **germs** in the spit make its prey sick enough to die.

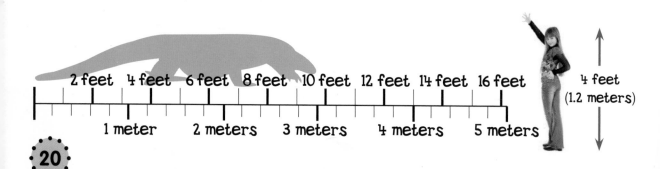

2 feet   4 feet   6 feet   8 feet   10 feet   12 feet   14 feet   16 feet   4 feet
(1.2 meters)

1 meter   2 meters   3 meters   4 meters   5 meters

Its **forked** tongue helps it smell its prey.

Female Komodo dragons dig out large **burrows** in sandy ground for their eggs. When the babies hatch, they live up in trees to avoid predators.

Python

Pythons live in Asia, Africa, New Guinea, and Australia. These snakes crawl on the land or up in the trees.

When hunting, pythons first strike with their long, curved teeth. Then they loop their bodies around their prey and squeeze hard. The animal cannot breathe and dies.

The **reticulated** python is the world's longest snake. Some have grown as long as 33 feet (10 meters.) They can swallow a deer whole.

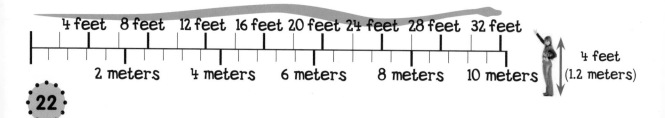

4 feet 8 feet 12 feet 16 feet 20 feet 24 feet 28 feet 32 feet

2 meters 4 meters 6 meters 8 meters 10 meters

4 feet (1.2 meters)

There are 26 known **species** of python. This royal python curls up into a ball to protect itself.

Python females lay fifteen to one hundred eggs. They curl themselves around the eggs and shiver to keep the eggs warm.

Rattlesnake

Rattlesnakes are poisonous. They bite their prey with long fangs that fold back up into their mouths. They hunt lizards, birds, and small animals, such as rats.

At the end of its tail is a rattle made of hard scales. A rattlesnake grows a new rattle every time it sheds its skin.

If a rattlesnake hears a person or animal nearby, it makes a buzzing noise with its rattle. The sound warns away predators.

4 feet
(1.2 meters)

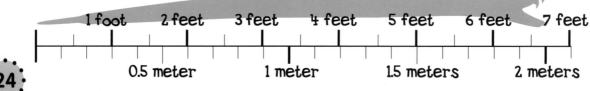

1 foot   2 feet   3 feet   4 feet   5 feet   6 feet   7 feet

0.5 meter   1 meter   1.5 meters   2 meters

This northern Pacific rattlesnake lives in deserts and other hot places in the United States.

Rattlesnakes are found from southern Canada to central Argentina. Many kinds live in the southern United States and Mexico.

Sea Turtle

Sea turtles swim though oceans all around the world. Most come on land only to lay their eggs.

Most sea turtles eat meat. But this green turtle lives on plants.

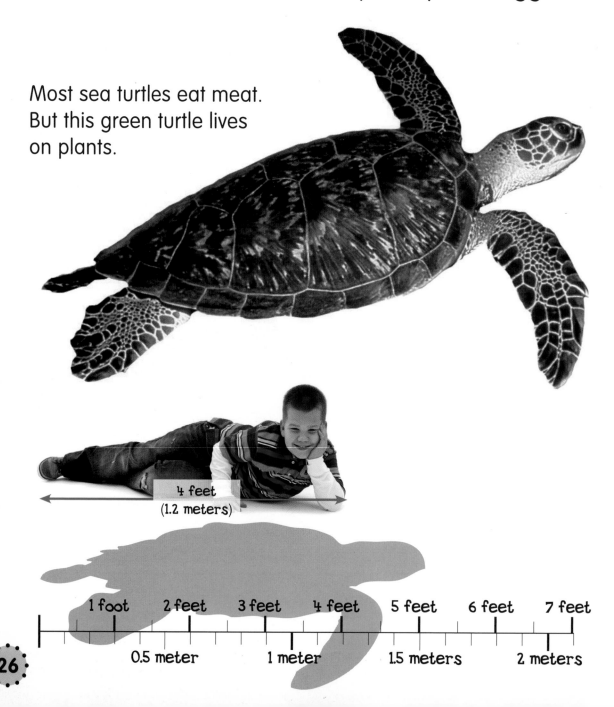

4 feet
(1.2 meters)

| 1 foot | 2 feet | 3 feet | 4 feet | 5 feet | 6 feet | 7 feet |

0.5 meter   1 meter   1.5 meters   2 meters

Female turtles crawl up on to a beach and dig a hole in the sand. There, they lay their eggs.

When the eggs hatch, the baby turtles have to run to the sea. Predators may attack them as they speed toward the water.

Thorny Devil Lizard

Thorny devils are lizards that live in hot deserts in Australia. They are strange, shy creatures.

Spikes grow all over the thorny devil's body. They protect it from predators.

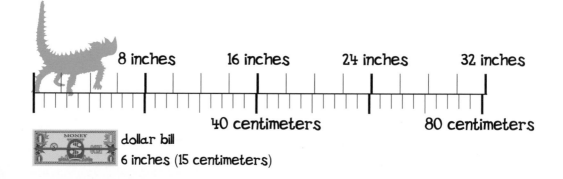

8 inches   16 inches   24 inches   32 inches

40 centimeters   80 centimeters

dollar bill
6 inches (15 centimeters)

Thorny devils eat ants.
They lick them up with their
tongues, one ant at a time.
They eat thousands of ants
in one meal.

Their gold and brown patches help
hide them in the desert sand.

For More Information

Books to Read

Bishop, Nic. *Lizards*. Scholastic, Inc.

Bredeson, Carmen. *Fun Facts About Snakes (I Like Reptiles and Amphibians)*. Enslow Elementary

Llewellyn, Claire. Explorers: *Reptiles*. Kingfisher

O'Neil, Amanda. *I Wonder Why Snakes Shed Their Skin and Other Questions about Reptiles*. Kingfisher

Pledger, Maurice. *Explore Reptiles*. Silver Dolphin Books

Simon, Seymour. *Giant Snakes (See More Readers)*. Chronicle Books

Places to Explore

Houston Zoo
6200 Hermann Park Drive
Houston, TX 77030
www.houstonzoo.org
Visit some of the world's largest snakes and lizards at the Reptile and Amphibian house.

Philadelphia Zoo
3400 W. Girard Avenue
Philadelphia, PA 19104
www.philadelphiazoo.org
Take a trip through rainforest and desert exhibits, and even watch a rain storm roll through the Everglades in the Reptile and Amphibian House.

Reptile Gardens
8955 S. Hwy 16
Rapid City, SD 57702
www.reptilegardens.com
Let famous conservationists introduce you to reptiles throughout their dome and gardens. The Reptile Gardens have more reptile species than any other zoo in the world.

Saint Louis Zoo
One Government Drive
St. Louis, MO 63110
www.stlzoo.org
Hang out with over 150 species of reptiles at both the Herpetarium and the Emerson Children's Zoo.

Web Sites to Visit

kids.nationalgeographic.com/kids/animals/creaturefeature/nile-crocodile
Discover crocodile facts and photos. Watch a Nile crocodile mother dig up her hatchlings and carry them in a pouch in her mouth to the river. You can also find information on other reptiles.

reptilesalive.com/kids/kids1scales.html
Learn how snakes shed their skins, experiment to find out what reptile eggs are like, and watch a video of a mother python twitching to keep her eggs warm.

video.nationalgeographic.com/video/player/kids/animals-pets-kids/reptiles-kids/chameleon-babies-kids.html
Come for chameleons, but stay for the baby loggerhead turtles and frilled lizard videos.

www.kidzone.ws/lw/snakes/facts.htm
Find pictures and learn how snakes move, how they use their special jaws, and what their armor and bones are like. Then enjoy snake riddles and printable worksheets.

Publisher's note: We have reviewed these Web sites to ensure that they are suitable for children. Web sites change frequently, however, so children should be closely supervised whenever they access the Internet.

Glossary

burrows — holes in the ground dug for shelter or protection

cacti — plural for *cactus*, which is a plant with a thick stem covered with spines instead of leaves. Cacti grow in deserts.

continents — huge sheets of rock floating on the surface of the earth. The seven large land areas on Earth are continents.

fangs — long, pointed teeth

forked — describes something with a divided end or branches

germs — tiny, living things, especially ones that cause illnesses

hatch — to break out of an egg

invertebrates — animals without backbones. Worms, insects, and shrimp are invertebrates.

islands — bodies of land that are completely surrounded by water. Islands are smaller than continents.

lizard — a type of reptile usually with four legs and a long body covered with scaly skin

mammals — animals that breathe air with their lungs, make their own body heat, produce milk for their babies, and have fur

nostrils — openings in the nose that take in and let out air

poison — something that can kill or hurt an animal or person

poisonous — describing something that can kill or hurt an animal or a person

predators — animals that hunt other creatures for food

prey — animals that are hunted for food

reticulated — marked with a pattern of lines that cross

rodents — small mammals with sharp teeth

scales — small stiff plates on the bodies of animals such as fish, lizards, and snakes

snakes — reptiles with long bodies covered with scales and no legs, arms, or wings

species — a group of living things of the same type

spikes — sharp, pointed growths on an animal's body

swamps — soft, wet areas of land

territory — the area where an animal lives. Animals guard their territories to stop other animals from eating the food in that area.

venom — the poison of some snakes, spiders, and other animals

Index